Collins

D1460973

SNAP REVISION WORKBOOK

AN INSPECTOR CALLS

GCSE 9-1 English Literature

For AQA

IAN KIRBY

BE EXAM-READY IN A SNAP

Published by Collins
An imprint of HarperCollins*Publishers*
1 London Bridge Street
London SE1 9GF

© HarperCollins*Publishers* Limited 2019

ISBN 9780008355265

First published 2019

10 9 8 7 6 5 4 3 2 1

British Library Cataloguing in Publication Data.
A CIP record of this book is available from the British Library.

Commissioning Editor: Claire Souza
Managing Editor: Shelley Teasdale
Author: Ian Kirby
Copyeditor and project management: Fiona Watson
Typesetting: Jouve India Private Limited
Cover designers: Kneath Associates and Sarah Duxbury
Illustrations: Rose and Thorn Creative Services Ltd
Production: Karen Nulty
Printed in the UK by Martins the Printer Ltd.

ACKNOWLEDGEMENTS

2,000 words from AN INSPECTOR CALLS AND OTHER PLAYS by J. B. Priestley (these plays first published by William Heinemann 1948-50, first published by Penguin Books 1969, Penguin Classics 2000). 'An Inspector Calls' copyright 1947 by J. B. Priestley.

The author and publisher are grateful to the copyright holders for permission to use quoted materials and images.

Every effort has been made to trace copyright holders and obtain their permission for the use of copyright material. The author and publisher will gladly receive information enabling them to rectify any error or omission in subsequent editions. All facts are correct at time of going to press.

MIX
Paper from
responsible source
FSC
www.fsc.org   FSC™ C007454

This book is produced from independently certified FSC™ paper to ensure responsible forest management.

For more information visit:
www.harpercollins.co.uk/green

Contents

Revise 1

Number the following events from the first half of Act 1 to show the correct order:

☐ The Inspector interrupts the Birlings' celebration to discuss Eva Smith's suicide.

☐ The Birlings are celebrating and are very happy.

☐ Discussing the suicide creates conflict between Mr Birling, Eric and the Inspector.

☐ The Inspector reveals that Eva was sacked from Mr Birling's factory.

Revise 2

Up to the point where Sheila meets the Inspector for the first time, what different things do we find out about the characters?

a) Mr Birling

b) Mrs Birling

c) Sheila

d) Eric

e) Gerald

Write one or two paragraphs analysing how the contrasting quotations below show the change in atmosphere on stage once the Inspector arrives.

> BIRLING: [beams at them and clearly relaxes] Well, well – this is very nice. Very nice.
>
> BIRLING: [rather angrily] Unless you brighten your ideas, you'll never be in a position to let anybody stay or tell anybody to go.

Look at this scene and fill in the missing key quotation.

WELL, WHAT IS IT THEN?

Look at Gerald's and Mr Birling's speech before and after the entrance of the Inspector. Commenting on dialogue and stage directions, write two or three paragraphs further exploring how the Inspector affects the atmosphere on stage.

Start making a record of the play's key moments and quotations. This could be a learning poster, a mobile, different cue cards or a changing screensaver on your phone or tablet. Keep developing it as you revise each act.

Revise 1

Number the following events from the second half of Act 1 to show the correct order:

☐ The Inspector reveals that Eva changed her name to Daisy Renton.

☐ Sheila admits that she had Eva sacked from Milwards.

☐ Gerald admits to Sheila that he had an affair with Daisy.

☐ Sheila criticises her father for sacking Eva from the factory.

Revise 2

What do the following quotations show about why Sheila had Eva sacked from Milwards?

a)

'… held the dress up, as if she was wearing it. And it just suited her. She was the right type for it, just as I was the wrong type.'

b)

'… I caught sight of this girl smiling at Miss Francis – as if to say: "Doesn't she look awful" – and I was absolutely furious.'

c)

'If she'd been some miserable plain little creature, I don't suppose I'd have done it. But she was very pretty and looked as if she could take care of herself.'

Write one or two paragraphs analysing how the contrasting quotations below, from the start and end of Act 1, show the change in Gerald and Sheila's relationship.

> SHEILA: Oh – it's wonderful! Look – Mummy – isn't it a beauty? Oh – darling – [She kisses Gerald hastily]
>
> SHEILA: Why – you fool – *he knows*. Of course he knows.

Look at this scene and fill in the missing key quotation.

ABOUT YOU AND THIS GIRL

YES. WE CAN KEEP IT FROM HIM.

Extend

Look at Gerald's interactions with Sheila at the start and end of Act 1. Commenting on his dialogue and the stage directions, write two or three paragraphs further exploring how the change in their relationship is shown.

Active Learning

Using Sheila's dialogue in Act 1 as a starting point, imagine when she has Eva sacked from Milwards and turn it into a small play scene or a comic strip.

Revise 1

Number the following events from the first half of Act 2 to show the correct order:

☐ Sheila gives her engagement ring back to Gerald.

☐ Gerald tries to get Sheila to leave the room.

☐ Gerald reveals the details of his affair with Daisy.

☐ Mrs Birling meets the Inspector for the first time and behaves in a superior manner.

Revise 2

Look at Gerald's dialogue where he explains about his first few meetings with Eva/Daisy. Select three short quotations and explain what they show about his feelings for the girl.

- ....

....

....

- ....

....

....

- ....

....

....

Revise 3

Write one or two paragraphs analysing how the following quotations show Mrs Birling's response to Gerald's affair. Relate your answer to the play's context.

INSPECTOR: And then you decided to keep her – as your mistress?

MRS BIRLING: What?

MRS BIRLING: I don't think we want any further details of this disgusting affair –

_____

_____

_____

_____

_____

_____

_____

Look at this scene and fill in the missing key quotation.

> ### Extend

Thinking about your answer to the Revise 3 task, write two or three paragraphs exploring how Sheila's responses to Gerald's affair are different to those of Mrs Birling. What does this suggest about the differences between Mrs Birling and Sheila?

> ### Active Learning

Create a mind map to show Sheila's thoughts after she returns the engagement ring. Consider how she feels about Gerald and the other characters at this point in the play.

Revise 1

Number the following events from the second half of Act 2 to show the correct order:

☐ The Inspector reveals that Eva was pregnant.

☐ Mr and Mrs Birling begin to realise that Eric was the father of Eva's child.

☐ Mrs Birling states that the father of Eva's child is responsible for her death.

☐ Mrs Birling admits that Eva appealed to her charitable organisation for help.

Revise 2

Explain how the following quotations from the end of Act 2 show that Sheila has worked out more about the situation than her mother.

a)

MRS BIRLING:	Certainly. And he ought to be dealt with very severely –
SHEILA:	[with sudden alarm] Mother – stop – stop!

b)

SHEILA:	[distressed] Now, Mother – don't you see?
MRS BIRLING:	[understanding now] But surely … I mean … it's ridiculous …

Look at the scene where the Inspector is questioning Mrs Birling. Write a paragraph analysing how her dialogue shows she treated Eva unfairly, and a paragraph exploring how she shows no regret for her actions. Relate your answer to the play's context.

Still focusing on the Inspector's questioning of Mrs Birling, write two or three paragraphs exploring Sheila's and the Inspector's reactions to Mrs Birling's responses. In what ways are they similar?

Continue your mind map from the first half of Act 2, considering how Sheila feels about her mother and father, the Inspector and Eva.

Look at this scene and fill in the missing key quotation.

> **Revise 1**

Number the following events from the first half of Act 3 to show the correct order:

☐ The Inspector reminds the Birling family that they are all responsible for Eva's death.

☐ Eric accuses Mrs Birling of killing Eva and her baby.

☐ As he leaves, the Inspector states that all members of society need to look after each other.

☐ Eric reveals how he met Eva and got her pregnant.

> **Revise 2**

Using the following quotations, explain how different characters respond to the truth about Eric and Eva.

a)

> MRS BIRLING: [with a cry] Oh – Eric – how could you?

b)

> BIRLING: [sharply] Sheila, take your mother along to the drawing-room –

c)

> INSPECTOR: Just used her for the end of a stupid drunken evening, as if she was an animal, a thing, not a person.

Write one or two paragraphs analysing how the following quotations convey the Inspector's final message to the Birlings. Relate your answer to the play's context.

> INSPECTOR: Remember what you did –
>
> INSPECTOR: We don't live alone. We are members of one body. We are responsible for each other.

Look at this scene and fill in the missing key quotation.

WHY DIDN'T YOU COME TO ME WHEN YOU FOUND YOURSELF IN THIS MESS?

Thinking about your answer to the Revise 3 task, look at the remainder of the Inspector's final speech and write two or three paragraphs exploring his message to the Birlings. What belief does he assert, what does he warn them about and how is this conveyed?

Make a poster, using words and images to convey the Inspector's beliefs about society.

Revise 1

Number the following events from the end of the play to show the correct order:

☐ Mr and Mrs Birling and Gerald relax and want to forget about the evening's events.

☐ The Birlings start to suspect that the Inspector isn't a real policeman.

☐ The Birlings receive a phone call from the police.

☐ When Gerald returns, he reveals that the Inspector isn't a real policeman.

Revise 2

Using the following quotations, explain what Mr Birling and Eric are thinking or feeling after the Inspector leaves.

a)

> BIRLING: There'll be a public scandal … I was almost certain for a knighthood in the next Honours List –

b)

> ERIC: You told us that a man has to make his own way, look after himself … that we weren't to take any notice of these cranks who tell us that everybody has to look after everybody else …

Write one or two paragraphs analysing how the following quotations show contrasting attitudes to the evening's events. Relate your answer to the play's context.

BIRLING: [Imitating Inspector] *You all helped to kill her.* [Pointing at Sheila and Eric and laughing.]

SHEILA: [passionately] You're pretending everything's just as it was before.

Extend

Thinking about your answer to the Revise 3 task, look at the end of the play, after Gerald telephones the hospital to confirm there hasn't been a suicide. Write two or three paragraphs exploring how Sheila and Eric are presented differently to Mr and Mrs Birling and Gerald.

Active Learning

Re-read the end of the play (from 'ERIC: And I agree with Sheila.'). Write what you imagine might be the next lines of dialogue spoken by each of the characters. Add explanations for each of your lines.

Look at this scene and fill in the missing key quotation.

IT FRIGHTENS ME THE WAY YOU TALK.

Revise 1

In what order are the five characters interrogated by the Inspector?

....

....

Revise 2

Explain the effect of the cliffhangers at the end of Acts 1 and 2. What plot ideas are they based around and how do they engage the audience?

a)

> SHEILA: I hate to think how much he knows that we don't know yet. You'll see. You'll see. [She looks at him almost in triumph.]
>
> [He looks crushed. The door slowly opens and the Inspector appears, looking steadily and searchingly at them.]
>
> INSPECTOR: Well?

....

....

....

....

....

b)

> MRS BIRLING: [agitated] I don't believe it. I *won't* believe it …
>
> SHEILA: Mother – I begged you and begged you to stop –
>
> [Inspector holds up a hand. We hear the front door. They wait, looking towards door. Eric enters, looking extremely pale and distressed. He meets their enquiring stares.]

....

....

....

....

....

Look at the end of the play (from 'GERALD: Everything's alright now, Sheila.') and analyse the effect of Priestley's final twist. Write two paragraphs on how the dialogue and stage directions change the atmosphere on stage, and what you think Priestley is trying to achieve.

Extend

Write two or three paragraphs that explore another point in the play where Priestley surprises the reader, such as Gerald's affair, Eva being pregnant or Eric being revealed as the father of Eva's baby. Consider the effects of dialogue and stage directions.

Active Learning

Create a tension graph for the play. Number the vertical axis from 1–10 and include the key moments along the horizontal axis, then plot where the tension rises and falls.

Look at this scene and fill in the missing key quotation.

Revise 1

Match the following terms with the correct definitions.

Socialism	Using someone unfairly for your (usually financial) benefit.
Capitalism	A belief in greater legal and financial equality and the importance of helping the poorest in society.
Exploitation	A belief in individual gain through hard work, the acceptance of inequality and the importance of profit.

Revise 2

In your own words, explain the following terms and link them to characters in *An Inspector Calls*:

a) Upper class

b) Middle class

c) Working class

Write one or two paragraphs analysing how Priestley presents class and politics in the following quotation. Consider how Birling is shown to be a middle-class capitalist, and how his opinions about socialism and the working class are presented.

> BIRLING: … just because the miners came out on strike, there's a lot of wild talk about possible labour trouble in the near future. Don't worry. We've past the worst of it. We employers at last are coming together to see that our interests – and the interests of Capital – are properly protected. And we're in for a time of steadily increasing prosperity.

Extend

Look at the section in Act 1 where the Inspector questions Mr Birling about his sacking of Eva Smith. Write two or three paragraphs exploring how Priestley presents Birling's views about capitalism and his workers.

Active Learning

To develop your understanding of the play's social and political setting, research the following topics:

a) The National Coal Strike 1912

b) Minimum Wage 1912

c) Trade Unions 1912.

Setting and Context

J.B. Priestley and 1945

Revise 1

Indicate whether the following statements about J.B. Priestley are true or false.

a) Priestley was born into a middle-class family. ....

b) Priestley didn't fight in the First World War. ....

c) Like his father, Priestley was a capitalist. ....

d) Priestley wrote the play in 1945. ....

e) Priestley's views about equality appear in the Inspector's dialogue. ....

Revise 2

Although the play's first audience were living in the 1940s, the play is set in 1912. Explain how Priestley uses the fact that his play is set in the past in the following quotations.

a)

> BIRLING: Why, a friend of mine went over this new liner last week – the *Titanic* … unsinkable, absolutely unsinkable.

....

....

....

b)

> BIRLING: In twenty or thirty years' time – let's say, in 1940 … there'll be peace and prosperity and rapid progress everywhere.

....

....

....

c)

> INSPECTOR: We are responsible for each other … if men will not learn that lesson, then they will be taught it in fire and blood and anguish.

....

....

....

Look at the Inspector's dialogue before he leaves in Act 3 (from 'And be quiet for a moment and listen to me' onwards). Focusing on the things he says to Mr and Mrs Birling, write one or two paragraphs analysing how Priestley's socialist views are presented through the Inspector.

Extend

Explore the second half of Act 3, after the Inspector leaves. How does Priestley use Sheila and Eric to present the rise in socialist beliefs amongst the younger generation (who might be watching the play, decades later in the 1940s)? Write two or three paragraphs, considering how Priestley suggests that their views are right, whereas those of their parents and Gerald are wrong.

Active Learning

To develop your understanding of the context in which J.B. Priestley was writing, research the following topics:

a) The Labour Government 1945

b) The Welfare State 1945.

Revise 1

Look at the Inspector's description of the lives of working-class girls like Eva Smith. What do the underlined phrases suggest about their lives?

> INSPECTOR: … these young women <u>counting their pennies</u> in their <u>dingy little</u> back bedrooms.

Revise 2

Explain what the following quotations suggest about the lives of working-class girls in 1912.

a)
> INSPECTOR: There are a lot of young women living that sort of existence in every city and big town in this country, Miss Birling. If there weren't, the factories and warehouses wouldn't know where to look for cheap labour.

b)
> GERALD: … she hadn't a penny and was going to be turned out of the miserable back room she had.

Look at the following quotation where Mrs Birling explains about her charitable work and why she didn't help Eva Smith. Write one or two paragraphs analysing how Priestley uses her words to criticise Christian morality in 1912.

> MRS BIRLING: We've done a great deal of useful work in helping deserving cases … I wasn't satisfied with the girl's claim – she seemed to me to be not a good case – and so I used my influence to have it refused.

Write two or three paragraphs exploring the other moral judgements that Mrs Birling makes during Act 2. Think about how she comments on Eva's life and her different responses during Gerald's story. How does Priestley also imply that, despite her moral judgements, she has no Christian values?

Using the internet, make a collage of images that show working-class life in 1912. You could add some quotations from the play that describe Eva's life. You could begin by using the search terms 'UK factories 1912' and 'UK living conditions 1912'.

Revise 1

During Act 1, Mr Birling's self-satisfied speech to Eric and Gerald is interrupted by '[the sharp ring of a front door bell]'. How might this be seen to represent the Inspector?

Revise 2

Explain the mood created on stage by the lighting that Priestley suggests in the following stage directions. Link each of your explanations to a piece of dialogue from Act 1.

a)
[The lighting should be pink and intimate until the Inspector arrives]

b)
[then it should be brighter and harder]

Write two paragraphs analysing how the setting of the Birlings' house (as described in the opening stage direction) tells us things about the family.

....

....

....

....

....

....

....

....

....

....

....

....

Extend

Think about your answer to the Revise 3 task. Write two or three paragraphs exploring how different dialogue from the Birling family in Act 1 can link to your different inferences about them from the description of the setting.

Active Learning

Re-read the opening stage directions, which describe the setting and the characters' costumes. Either draw a picture to show how this may look on stage or use the internet to research different sets that have been used for past productions of the play.

Revise 1

Look at how the Inspector describes Eva Smith's life to Sheila. Underline five words or phrases that show the Inspector's sympathy for Eva's situation.

> INSPECTOR: She was out of work for the next two months. Both her parents were dead, so that she'd no home to go back to. And she hadn't been able to save much out of what Birling and Company had paid her. So that after two months, with no work, no money coming in, and living in lodgings, with no relatives to help her, few friends, lonely, half-starved, she was feeling desperate.

Revise 2

How is Inspector Goole presented in the following quotations from Act 1?

a)

> BIRLING: Sit down, Inspector.
>
> INSPECTOR: Thank you, sir.

b)

> BIRLING: But I don't understand why you should come here, Inspector –
>
> INSPECTOR: [Cutting through, massively] I've been round to the room she had, and she'd left a letter there and a sort of diary.

c)

> BIRLING: If you don't come down sharply on some of these people, they'd soon be asking for the earth.
>
> GERALD: I should say so!
>
> INSPECTOR: They might. But after all it's better to ask for the earth than to take it.

Look at the second half of Act 1, where the Inspector is questioning Sheila about how she treated Eva at Milwards. Write a paragraph analysing how the Inspector takes control of the situation and a paragraph analysing how he makes Sheila feel guilty.

Look at this scene and fill in the missing key quotation.

I'M NOT GOING TO HAVE THIS, INSPECTOR. YOU'LL APOLOGISE AT ONCE.

Extend

Look at the second half of Act 2, where the Inspector is questioning Mrs Birling. Write two or three paragraphs exploring how Priestley uses dialogue and stage directions to present the Inspector. Refer to the play's context within your answer.

Active Learning

Write an interview with the Inspector where he is asked for his opinions about the Birlings and their attitudes towards other people.

Revise 1

Look at Birling's speech in Act 1 after Gerald gives Sheila the engagement ring (from 'I just want to say this' to where Mrs Birling, Sheila and Eric exit). Select a quotation to show each of the following aspects of Birling's character:

a) He is dominant.

b) He is self-important.

c) He is patronising.

d) He has capitalist values.

e) He doesn't understand the world as well as he thinks he does.

Revise 2

Focusing on Act 1, select and explain a quotation that shows Birling's feelings or attitudes towards the different members of his family.

a) Mrs Birling

b) Sheila

c) Eric

Using the following quotations from Act 1, and referring to the play's context, write two paragraphs exploring how Priestley presents different aspects of Birling's social status.

> 'I have an idea that your mother – Lady Croft – while she doesn't object to my girl – feels you might have done better for yourself socially –'
>
> 'I was Lord Mayor here two years ago when Royalty visited us.'
>
> '… there's a very good chance of a knighthood – so long as we behave ourselves, don't get into the police court or start a scandal – eh? [Laughs complacently]'

Extend

Look at Birling's interactions with his children in Act 3. Write two or three paragraphs exploring how Priestley uses dialogue and stage directions to present Birling's attitudes towards his children. Refer to the play's context within your answer.

Active Learning

Create a learning poster to explore how Mr Birling conflicts with Inspector Goole.

Sketch the two men's faces in the centre of the poster. On one side, note down quotations that show Birling's attitudes or beliefs and how he behaves towards the Inspector. On the other side, add quotations that show the Inspector's contrasting attitudes or beliefs and how he responds to Birling. Use one colour for attitudes/beliefs and another colour for behaviour. Where possible, use arrows to show direct links between your ideas.

Look at this scene and fill in the missing key quotation.

HEAR, HEAR! AND I THINK MY FATHER WOULD AGREE TO THAT.

Revise 1

Using the words below, fill in the gaps in this paragraph analysing how Mrs Birling is presented at the start of Act 2.

have priority   more important   dismissive   working class

'that class'   verb   young people   empathise

Mrs Birling sees herself as _____ than other people. She places herself above

_____ and the _____ when speaking to Sheila: 'Please don't

contradict me like that. And in any case I don't suppose for a moment that we can understand why the

girl committed suicide. Girls of that class –'. The _____ 'contradict' shows she believes her views

_____ while the phrase _____ indicates disapproval of the poor. She is

_____ of Eva's suicide, convinced it has nothing to do with her family, and the phrase 'I don't

suppose for a moment that we can understand' suggests her unwillingness to _____ with others.

Revise 2

Look at the following lines from Act 2, where Mrs Birling is being questioned by the Inspector. Comment on the effect of the words or phrases in bold.

a)

'We've done a great deal of useful work in helping **deserving** cases.'

b)

'... that was one of the things that **prejudiced** me against her case.'

c)

'**I'm very sorry**. **But** I think she had only **herself to blame**.'

d)

> 'She was giving herself **ridiculous airs**. She was **claiming elaborate fine feelings and scruples** that were simply **absurd in a girl in her position**.'

Look at Mrs Birling's different comments during Gerald's confession in Act 2. Write two paragraphs exploring what her reactions show about her. Link your ideas to the play's context.

Look at the gradual revelation that Eric got Eva pregnant (from 'INSPECTOR: Who is to blame then?' towards the end of Act 2, to 'MRS BIRLING: No – Eric – please – I didn't know – didn't understand –' in Act 3).

Write two or three paragraphs exploring how Priestley uses dialogue and stage directions to present the repercussions of Mrs Birling's uncompromising and judgemental attitudes. Refer to the play's context within your answer.

Look at this scene and fill in the missing key quotation.

Construct an illustrated axis of power for Mrs Birling. Select 12 quotations that show Mrs Birling at different stages throughout the play (four from each act). Arrange them along a line to show when she is most in control and least in control. Add a sketch for each quotation to represent what is happening and what she is feeling.

You might begin with, 'All right, Edna. I'll ring from the drawing room when we want coffee.' How much power and control does this show?

Revise 1

Look at Sheila's response when she first hears that a girl has committed suicide.

> 'It's just that I can't help thinking about this girl – destroying herself so horribly – and I've been so happy tonight. Oh, I wish you hadn't told me. What was she like? Quite young?'

Underline the following features of Sheila's speech:

a) An adverb that suggests she is sympathetic.

b) A phrase that makes her sound selfish.

c) A phrase where she compares her life to the girl's.

d) A sentence that shows her curiosity.

Revise 2

a) Explain what later events in the play are foreshadowed by the following lines spoken by Sheila in Act 1.

   i)
   > SHEILA: Yes – except for all last summer, when you never came near me, and I wondered what had happened to you.

   ....

   ....

   ii)
   > MRS BIRLING: When you're married you'll realise that men with important work to do sometimes have to spend nearly all their time and energy on their business. You'll have to get used to that …
   >
   > SHEILA: I don't believe I will.

   ....

   ....

b) What is Priestley trying to show about the Birlings through this foreshadowing?

   ....

   ....

   ....

   ....

Look at the second half of Act 1, after Sheila first meets the Inspector. Write a paragraph exploring how Sheila criticises her father and a paragraph exploring how she both accepts and avoids responsibility for Eva's death.

_____

_____

_____

_____

_____

_____

_____

Look at this scene and fill in the missing key quotation.

I DON'T LIKE YOUR TONE NOR THE WAY YOU'RE HANDLING THIS INQUIRY, AND I DON'T INTEND TO GIVE YOU MUCH MORE ROPE.

YOU NEEDN'T GIVE ME ANY ROPE.

Extend

Focus on Sheila in Act 2. Write two or three paragraphs exploring how Priestley uses dialogue and stage directions to show her increasing guilt for how she and her family affected Eva Smith's life. Refer to the play's context within your answer.

Active Learning

Create a learning poster to show the different sides of Sheila's character.

Sketch how you imagine Sheila looks. On one side of the poster, add quotations that show the selfish and self-satisfied side of her character. On the other, include quotations to exemplify her acceptance of guilt and greater empathy for others. You could also add small sketches to represent key scenes in the play that relate to Sheila's character.

Revise 1

Find quotations from the first half of Act 1 that show the following things about Eric's character:

a) He's a little immature and squabbles with Sheila.

b) He drinks too much.

c) He struggles to assert himself with his father.

d) He tends to do what his parents tell him.

Revise 2

Explain what the following quotations show about Eric and his relationship with Eva.

a)

> '… afterwards she told me she didn't want me to go in but that – well, I was in that state when a chap easily turns nasty – and I threatened to make a row.'

b)

> 'I wasn't in love with her or anything – but I liked her – she was pretty and a good sport –'

c)

> '… I insisted on giving her enough money to keep her going – until she refused to take any more –'

Using the following quotations, explore how Eric comes into conflict with his family. Write a paragraph focusing on Sheila and a paragraph focusing on his mother.

> (About Eric's drinking)
>
> ERIC: *You* told her. Why, you little sneak!
>
> SHEILA: No, that's not fair, Eric. I could have told her months ago, but of course I didn't.

> ERIC: She came to you to protect me – and you turned her away – yes, and you killed her – and the child she'd have had, too – my child – your own grandchild – you killed them both – damn you, damn you –

....

....

....

....

....

....

....

Look at this scene and fill in the missing key quotation.

I DON'T WANT ANY OF THAT TALK FROM YOU –

Extend

Look at Eric's interactions with Mr Birling in Act 3. Write two or three paragraphs exploring how Priestley uses dialogue and stage directions to present Eric's relationship with his father. Refer to the play's context within your answer.

Active Learning

'And this time we talked a bit. She told me something about herself and I talked too.'

Write a conversation between Eva and Eric, imagining what he would tell her about himself and his relationship with his family.

Revise 1

Look at the section of Act 1 where Birling explains to the Inspector about how he responded to the factory workers going on strike.

Select three quotations that suggest Gerald has similar values to Mr Birling and agrees with his treatment of the workers.

Revise 2

Look at the following quotations from Act 2 about Gerald's affair with Eva/Daisy. Explain what each one shows about his feelings for her. Consider where his treatment of her is both positive and negative.

a)

'All she wanted was to talk – a little friendliness – and I gathered that Joe Meggarty's advances had left her rather shaken –'

b)

'… she was desperately hard up and at that moment was actually hungry. I made the people at the County find some food for her.'

c)

'… I didn't install her there so I could make love to her. I made her go to Morgan Terrace because I was sorry for her …'

d)

'She told me she'd been happier than she'd ever been before – but that she knew it couldn't last – hadn't expected it to last.'

Looking at Act 1 from the point where Inspector Goole is introduced, explore Gerald's attitude towards the Inspector. Write a paragraph focusing on how he is dismissive of the investigation and a paragraph focusing on how he defends himself or thinks himself above the Inspector.

Extend

SHEILA: You and I aren't the same people who sat down to dinner here.

Look at Gerald and Sheila's interactions in Act 2. Write two or three paragraphs exploring how Priestley uses dialogue and stage directions to present their relationship deteriorating. Refer to the play's context within your answer.

Look at this scene and fill in the missing key quotation.

SOMETIMES THERE ISN'T AS MUCH DIFFERENCE AS YOU THINK.

Active Learning

Make a learning poster evaluating how far Gerald is to blame for Eva's suicide. Draw an image of the scales of justice. Above one scale, note down the things that Gerald does to help Eva. Add the things he does that have a negative effect on her life to the other scale. Consider the relevance of his different thoughts and feelings about Eva.

Support your ideas with evidence from the text.

Revise 1

> INSPECTOR: This girl killed herself – and died a horrible death. But each of you helped to kill her.

Summarise the different ways that Mr Birling, Sheila, Mrs Birling, Gerald and Eric contributed to Eva Smith's death.

_____

_____

_____

_____

Revise 2

Looking at the following quotations, explain the different attitudes that the Birlings and the Inspector have towards Eva Smith.

> INSPECTOR: ... what happened to her afterwards may have driven her to suicide. A chain of events.
>
> MR BIRLING: ... I can't accept any responsibility. If we were all responsible for everything that happened to everybody we'd had anything to do with, it would be very awkward, wouldn't it?

> MRS BIRLING: She was claiming elaborate fine feelings and scruples that were simply absurd in a girl in her position.
>
> INSPECTOR: [very sternly] Her position now is that she lies with a burnt-out inside on a slab.

_____

_____

_____

_____

_____

_____

_____

Look at the sections in Act 1 and Act 2 where Mr and Mrs Birling are questioned by the Inspector. Explore how their responses show the power that they had over Eva Smith. Write one paragraph about Mr Birling and one paragraph about Mrs Birling. Link your comments to the play's context.

Look at this scene and fill in the missing key quotation.

Think about the different things that the audience is told about Eva Smith and how her life has been affected by others. Write two or three paragraphs exploring how Priestley uses language to create sympathy for Eva. Refer to the play's context within your answer.

Create an illustrated timeline for Eva Smith's life, adding sketches and quotations to show how her life was affected by the other characters in the play.

Revise 1

Look at the following extract from the Inspector's final speech. Focusing on the phrases in bold, in what way does he want people like the Birlings to change?

> 'One Eva Smith has gone – but **there are millions and millions and millions of Eva Smiths** and John Smiths still left with us, with their lives, their hopes and fears, **their suffering and chance of happiness**, all intertwined with our lives, with **what we think and say and do**. We don't live alone. **We are members of one body. We are responsible for each other**.'

Revise 2

Using the following quotations, explain how far each member of the Birling family changes their outlook on life due to the Inspector's investigation.

a)

> MRS BIRLING: He certainly didn't make me *confess* – as you call it. I told him quite plainly that I thought I had done no more than my duty.

b)

> MR BIRLING: Probably a Socialist or some sort of crank – he talked like one.

c)

> SHEILA: I behaved badly too. I know I did. I'm ashamed of it. But now you're beginning all over again to pretend that nothing much has happened.

d)

> ERIC: ... do you remember what you said to Gerald and me after dinner, when you were feeling so pleased with yourself? You told us that a man has to make his own way ...

Look at Mr Birling's interactions with Eric once the Inspector has left. Explore how Mr Birling is presented as unchanged by the night's events. Write a paragraph about how he avoids guilt for Eva's death and a paragraph considering how he selfishly focuses on the consequences to his own life.

_____

_____

_____

_____

_____

_____

_____

Look at this scene and fill in the missing key quotation.

AND I CAN'T SEE IT LIKE THAT. THIS GIRL'S STILL DEAD, ISN'T SHE? NOBODY'S BROUGHT HER TO LIFE, HAVE THEY?

THAT'S JUST WHAT I FEEL, ERIC. AND IT'S WHAT THEY DON'T SEEM TO UNDERSTAND.

SHEILA: Between us we drove that girl to commit suicide.

Think about the end of the play, after Mr Birling has telephoned the Chief Constable and discovered that Inspector Goole isn't a real policeman. Write two or three paragraphs exploring how Priestley uses language and stage directions to show to what extent the characters have been changed by their experience. Refer to the play's context within your answer.

Create a learning poster to illustrate how far each character changes. On the left side of your poster, sketch the characters' faces and note down their attitudes to others and how they affected Eva's life. On the right side, comment on how far their attitudes have changed and how much responsibility they accept for Eva's death. Include key quotations and use shading or different colours to represent the degree of change.

Revise 1

Look at the following description of Alderman Meggarty and underline the words that suggest that, despite being a respected town councillor, he lacks morality.

> GERALD: Old Joe Meggarty, half-drunk and goggle-eyed … He's a notorious womaniser as well as being one of the worst sots and rogues in Brumley.

Revise 2

Explain which characters are linked to the seven deadly sins and why.

a) Envy

b) Gluttony

c) Greed

d) Lust

e) Pride

f) Sloth

g) Wrath

Using the following quotation from Act 1, write one or two paragraphs analysing how Priestley presents different attitudes to morality. Refer to the play's context.

> GERALD: … we're respectable citizens and not criminals.
>
> INSPECTOR: Sometimes there isn't as much difference as you think.

Look at this scene and fill in the missing key quotation.

Extend

Write two or three paragraphs exploring how Priestley challenges attitudes to morality through the Inspector's questioning of Mrs Birling in the second half of Act 2.

Active Learning

Create a visual representation of the seven deadly sins, linking them to the characters in the play through quotations and images. You could even design it in the shape of a pie chart, evaluating which of the characters' sins had most of an effect on Eva.

Revise 1

Look at the following quotation. Explain how the words in bold show the consequences of society having a survival of the fittest attitude.

> INSPECTOR: This afternoon a **young** woman drank some disinfectant, and **died**, after several hours of **agony** … She felt she **couldn't go on** any longer.

Revise 2

Explain how the quotations below show Mr Birling's survival of the fittest attitude.

a)

> MR BIRLING: … a man has to make his own way – has to look after himself –

b)

> MR BIRLING: … as if we were all mixed up together like bees in a hive – community and all that nonsense.

Look at the Inspector's final speech before he leaves in Act 3. Analyse how Priestley uses the Inspector to argue against the idea of survival of the fittest. Refer to the play's context within your answer.

Look at this scene and fill in the missing key quotation.

A GIRL DIED TONIGHT. A PRETTY, LIVELY SORT OF GIRL, WHO NEVER DID ANYBODY ANY HARM.

DON'T PLEASE – I KNOW, I KNOW – AND I CAN'T STOP THINKING ABOUT IT –

Extend

Focusing on Act 1, write two or three paragraphs exploring another moment where Priestley uses the Inspector to argue against the idea of survival of the fittest.

Create a learning poster exploring Mr Birling's and the Inspector's opposing views about survival of the fittest.

Revise 1

Write a definition of 'social responsibility'.

Revise 2

Looking at the following quotations, explain how Mr Birling and the Inspector have different views about social responsibility.

a)

> MR BIRLING: But the way some of these cranks talk and write now, you'd think everybody has to look after everybody else.

b)

> INSPECTOR: ... it would do us all a bit of good if sometimes we tried to put ourselves in the place of these young women ...

Using the following quotations, write two paragraphs analysing how Priestley presents the importance of social responsibility. Refer to the play's context within your answer.

> INSPECTOR: … we'll have to share our guilt.
>
> INSPECTOR: She needed not only money, but advice, sympathy, friendliness.

Look at this scene and fill in the missing key quotation.

MOTHER, I THINK IT WAS CRUEL AND VILE.

Write two or three paragraphs exploring how Gerald shows a lack of social responsibility in Act 3.

Imagine Sheila is asked what she has learnt about social responsibility from the Inspector's investigation. Write a short speech expressing how and why her views have changed.

Revise 1

Write a definition of 'personal responsibility'.

Revise 2

Look at the following quotations. Explain how the words or phrases in bold show different aspects of personal responsibility.

a)

> BIRLING: You're the one I **blame** for this.

b)

> ERIC: … the **fact** remains that **I did what I did**.

c)

> SHEILA: And don't let's start **dodging and pretending** now. **Between us we** drove that girl to commit suicide.

Look at Sheila's speech after the Inspector leaves in Act 3 (beginning, 'I'm going anyhow in a minute or two'). Write two paragraphs analysing how Priestley shows Sheila accepting, and trying to get others to accept, personal responsibility.

_____

_____

_____

_____

_____

_____

_____

_____

_____

_____

Look at this scene and fill in the missing key quotation.

Extend

Focusing on Mr Birling, Mrs Birling or Gerald in Act 3, write two or three paragraphs exploring how Priestley shows a character avoiding personal responsibility.

Active Learning

In Act 3, the Inspector says, 'You can't even say "I'm sorry, Eva Smith".' Imagine Sheila or Eric had the opportunity to apologise. Write a small speech or letter from their point of view, accepting their personal responsibility for what they did to her.

Revise 1

Looking at Act 1, make a list of quotations that reflect the Birlings' social status. Consider:

- the initial stage directions
- Mr Birling's job, power and roles in the community
- who Mrs Birling gives orders to
- Eric's upbringing
- Sheila's economic power.

Revise 2

Explain what the following quotation suggests about Mr Birling's view of inequality.

> BIRLING: … if I'd agreed to this demand for a new rate we'd have added about twelve percent to our labour costs. … If you don't come down sharply on some of these people, they'd soon be asking for the earth.

Look back at Act 2 where Gerald describes how he got to know Eva/Daisy. Analyse how Priestley contrasts Gerald's and Eva's lifestyles in order to present inequality. Refer to the play's context in your answer.

....

....

....

....

....

....

....

....

....

Look at this scene and fill in the missing key quotation.

THERE ARE A LOT OF YOUNG WOMEN LIVING THAT SORT OF EXISTENCE IN EVERY CITY AND BIG TOWN IN THIS COUNTRY, MISS BIRLING. IF THERE WEREN'T, THE FACTORIES AND WAREHOUSES WOULDN'T KNOW WHERE TO LOOK FOR CHEAP LABOUR. ASK YOUR FATHER.

Extend

Write two or three paragraphs exploring one moment from the play where the Inspector tries to make another character understand what Eva Smith's life was like. How does Priestley use language to convey ideas about inequality?

Active Learning

Considering the difference between 'a fairly large suburban house' and 'dingy little back bedrooms', imagine the contrasting living conditions of the Birlings and Eva Smith and draw a picture that represents the inequality in the play.

Revise 1

Explain how this extract from Act 1 presents a typical image of adults and youngsters in a family.

SHEILA:	You're squiffy.
ERIC:	I'm not.
MRS BIRLING:	What an expression, Sheila! Really, the things you girls pick up these days!
ERIC:	If you think that's the best she can do –
SHEILA:	Don't be an ass, Eric.
MRS BIRLING:	Now stop it, you two.

Revise 2

Looking at Act 1, before the Inspector arrives, select one moment where Mr Birling interrupts and patronises Eric, and one moment where he demands Sheila's attention. Explain your choices.

Look at Act 3, before the Inspector leaves. Analyse a moment where Priestley shows Eric coming into conflict with his parents, and a moment where Sheila conflicts with her parents. Write a paragraph for each and refer to the play's context.

Extend

Looking at Act 3, after the Inspector leaves, write two or three paragraphs exploring another moment where Sheila and Eric come into conflict with their parents. How does Priestley convey the conflict and what positive message is he trying to suggest about the younger generation?

Active Learning

Create a learning poster to show how and why the younger generation's attitudes towards their parents change in the play.

Look at this scene and fill in the missing key quotation.

AND I SAY – EITHER STOP SHOUTING OR GET OUT.

Revise 1

Why do you think Priestley chose to set his play in 'real time' over one evening? How does it affect the mood on stage?

Revise 2

Select and explain evidence that shows how characters respond to the past.

a) Sheila's distress at the effects of her past behaviour.

b) Gerald's desperation to keep his past secret.

c) Mrs Birling's shock at her son's past.

d) Mr Birling's fear that the past could cause a scandal.

Look at Act 3, after the Inspector has left. Write a paragraph analysing how Priestley presents Mrs Birling as wanting to deny that she has done anything wrong in the past, and a paragraph on how Sheila is shown wanting to accept her past actions.

_____

_____

_____

_____

_____

_____

_____

_____

Look at this scene and fill in the missing key quotation.

Write two or three paragraphs exploring how Priestley uses the Inspector's dialogue and stage directions throughout the play to suggest the importance of the past.

Create a poster titled 'A chain of events', illustrating the ways in which the different actions of the characters interlink and lead to Eva's suicide.

Revise 1

Although it opens with an engagement, in what different ways can the play be said to present a *lack* of love?

....

....

....

Revise 2

Look at the following quotations from Act 1. Thinking about how Priestley uses foreshadowing, explain how these references to Gerald and Sheila's relationship link to later events in the play.

a)

> GERALD: And I've told you – I was awfully busy at the works all that time.
>
> SHEILA: Yes, that's what *you* say.

....

....

....

b)

> GERALD: And I drink to you – and hope I can make you as happy as you deserve to be.

....

....

....

c)

> MRS BIRLING: It's a lovely ring. Be careful with it.
>
> SHEILA: Careful! I'll never let it go out of my sight for an instant.

....

....

....

Look at Gerald's description of his relationship with Eva/Daisy in Act 2. Write two paragraphs analysing how Priestley presents Gerald's attitude towards the relationship in comparison to Eva's/Daisy's attitude. Refer to the play's context in your answer.

_____

_____

_____

_____

_____

_____

_____

_____

Extend

Look at Acts 2 and 3. Write two or three paragraphs exploring Gerald's attitude to his relationship with Sheila once he has admitted to his affair with Eva/Daisy. How and why does Mr Birling try to support Gerald?

Active Learning

Create a learning poster showing the different reasons Mr Birling has for approving of Sheila's engagement to Gerald.

Look at this scene and fill in the missing key quotation.

NO, NOT YET. IT'S TOO SOON. I MUST THINK.

How does Priestley present the Inspector as an unusual character in the play?

Write about:

- the ways the Inspector behaves and speaks to people
- how Priestley presents the Inspector by the way he writes.

Revise 1

Underline the words or phrases that show what you need to focus on to successfully answer the question.

Revise 2

Plan your response to the question. Try to come up with three to five ideas, linked to quotations and contextual references.

Write an introduction to your answer, giving a clear overview of the question and your approach to it. Then write up your first point. Spend a maximum of 15 minutes on this task.

Finish off your response to the question, using the time you have remaining from the allocated 45 minutes.

'In *An Inspector Calls*, Arthur Birling isn't used to being challenged.' Explore how far you agree with this statement.

Write about:

- how Priestley presents the character of Arthur Birling
- how Priestley uses the character of Arthur Birling to explore some of his ideas.

Revise 1

Underline the words or phrases that show what you need to focus on to successfully answer the question.

Revise 2

Plan your response to the question. Try to come up with three to five ideas, linked to quotations and contextual references.

Write an introduction to your answer, giving a clear overview of the question and your approach to it. Then write up your first point. Spend a maximum of 15 minutes on this task.

Extend

Finish off your response to the question, using the time you have remaining from the allocated 45 minutes.

How does Priestley present the relationship between Gerald and Sheila in the play?

Write about:

- what Sheila and Gerald's relationship is like
- how Priestley presents the relationship by the way he writes.

Revise 1

Underline the words or phrases that show what you need to focus on to successfully answer the question.

Revise 2

Plan your response to the question. Try to come up with three to five ideas, linked to quotations and contextual references.

Write an introduction to your answer, giving a clear overview of the question and your approach to it. Then write up your first point. Spend a maximum of 15 minutes on this task.

Extend

Finish off your response to the question, using the time you have remaining from the allocated 45 minutes.

How does Priestley use the character of Mrs Birling to explore ideas about morality in the play?

Write about:

- how Priestley presents Mrs Birling
- how Priestley uses Mrs Birling to present some of his ideas.

Revise 1

Underline the words or phrases that show what you need to focus on to successfully answer the question.

Revise 2

Plan your response to the question. Try to come up with three to five ideas, linked to quotations and contextual references.

Write an introduction to your answer, giving a clear overview of the question and your approach to it. Then write up your first point. Spend a maximum of 15 minutes on this task.

Extend

Finish off your response to the question, using the time you have remaining from the allocated 45 minutes.

How does Priestley present attitudes towards responsibility in the play?

Write about:

- what some of the attitudes towards responsibility are
- how Priestley presents some of these attitudes by the way he writes.

Revise 1

Underline the words or phrases that show what you need to focus on to successfully answer the question.

Revise 2

Plan your response to the question. Try to come up with three to five ideas, linked to quotations and contextual references.

Write an introduction to your answer, giving a clear overview of the question and your approach to it. Then write up your first point. Spend a maximum of 15 minutes on this task.

Extend

Finish off your response to the question, using the time you have remaining from the allocated 45 minutes.

An Inspector Calls has been described as 'a play about inequality'. To what extent do you agree with this view?

Write about:

- how Priestley presents inequality
- how Priestley uses inequality to explore some of his ideas about society.

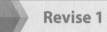

Revise 1

Underline the words or phrases that show what you need to focus on to successfully answer the question.

Revise 2

Plan your response to the question. Try to come up with three to five ideas, linked to quotations and contextual references.

Write an introduction to your answer, giving a clear overview of the question and your approach to it. Then write up your first point. Spend a maximum of 15 minutes on this task.

Extend

Finish off your response to the question, using the time you have remaining from the allocated 45 minutes.

How does Priestley use the Birlings to explore ideas about respectability in the play?

Write about:

- what ideas Priestley presents about respectability
- how Priestley presents these ideas through the way he writes.

Revise 1

Underline the words or phrases that show what you need to focus on to successfully answer the question.

Revise 2

Plan your response to the question. Try to come up with three to five ideas, linked to quotations and contextual references.

Write an introduction to your answer, giving a clear overview of the question and your approach to it. Then write up your first point. Spend a maximum of 15 minutes on this task.

Extend

Finish off your response to the question, using the time you have remaining from the allocated 45 minutes.

An Inspector Calls has been described as 'a play about secrets and lies'. To what extent do you agree with this view?

Write about:

- how Priestley presents secrets and lies
- how Priestley uses secrets and lies to explore some of his ideas about society.

> ### Revise 1
>
> Underline the words or phrases that show what you need to focus on to successfully answer the question.

> ### Revise 2
>
> Plan your response to the question. Try to come up with three to five ideas, linked to quotations and contextual references.

Write an introduction to your answer, giving a clear overview of the question and your approach to it. Then write up your first point. Spend a maximum of 15 minutes on this task.

Extend

Finish off your response to the question, using the time you have remaining from the allocated 45 minutes.

Answers

Pages 4–5

Revise 1

1) The Birlings are celebrating and are very happy.
2) The Inspector interrupts the Birlings' celebration to discuss Eva Smith's suicide.
3) The Inspector reveals that Eva was sacked from Mr Birling's factory.
4) Discussing the suicide creates conflict between Mr Birling, Eric and the Inspector.

Revise 2

Answers should include:

a) Mr Birling: prosperous businessman; made money rather than born into it; dominant; over-confident; wants more social status.
b) Mrs Birling: higher class than her husband; believes in etiquette; believes women have their place in a family.
c) Sheila: engaged to Gerald; a little spoilt and childish; bickers with Eric; light-hearted.
d) Eric: doesn't seem to fit in; slightly drunk; tries but fails to stand up to his father; cares about people more than the others.
e) Gerald: higher class than the Birlings (son of Lady Croft); father is a wealthy businessman; often agrees with Mr Birling.

Revise 3

Answers might explore: the change in Birling's tone of voice and body language, as suggested by the stage directions; the change from Birling's positive language about the evening to his criticism of Eric; the repetition and pauses in the first quotation, suggesting calm, compared to the long attack in the second.

Comic Strip

'I'd like some information, if you don't mind, Mr Birling.'

Extend

Answers might explore: Birling's and Gerald's private joke about the knighthood, and Birling's language of contentment and confidence before the Inspector's arrival, contrasted with Birling's impatience, Gerald's annoyance, and the way in which they are interrogated by the Inspector but don't have their own questions answered.

Pages 6–7

Revise 1

1) Sheila criticises her father for sacking Eva from the factory.
2) Sheila admits that she had Eva sacked from Milwards.
3) The Inspector reveals that Eva changed her name to Daisy Renton.
4) Gerald admits to Sheila that he had an affair with Daisy.

Revise 2

Answers should include: a) she was angry that a dress didn't suit her and jealous that it could have suited Eva; b) she felt the girl was mocking her and wanted to get her own back (she may also have disliked being mocked by someone of a lower class); c) she was jealous of the girl's prettiness and didn't feel any sympathy for her.

Revise 3

Analysis might include: the change from happiness to tension; Sheila's use of the word 'darling' and the stage direction '[kisses]' showing love, contrasted with her criticism of Gerald ('you fool'); Sheila's use of 'wonderful' to show her approval of Gerald's choices, compared to her correcting and contradicting him when she says *'he knows. Of course he knows'*; the context of them getting engaged and the more serious context of being investigated and knowing he's had an affair.

Comic Strip

So – for God's sake – don't say anything to the Inspector.

Extend

Answers might explore: the relaxed, loving attitude towards Sheila and his wish to make her happy, contrasted with how he tries to keep the affair secret from the Inspector, his silences and his concern more for his own reputation than his relationship with Sheila.

Pages 8–9

Revise 1

1) Gerald tries to get Sheila to leave the room.
2) Mrs Birling meets the Inspector for the first time and behaves in a superior manner.
3) Gerald reveals the details of his affair with Daisy.
4) Sheila gives her engagement ring back to Gerald.

Revise 2

Answers might include: 'young and fresh and charming' – shows his initial attraction; 'obviously she wasn't enjoying herself' – shows sympathy; 'asked her questions about herself' – shows his interest in her; 'she was desperately hard up … actually hungry' – shows pity; 'insisted on Daisy moving into those rooms and I made her take some money' – shows his wish to help.

Revise 3

Answers might focus on: her shock at finding Gerald kept a mistress, partly linked to how she thinks people of a higher class behave better than that, and her dislike of the affair, shown in the adjective 'disgusting' and her wish to bring the topic to an end.

Comic Strip

'we'll have to share our guilt.'

Extend

Answers might explore: unlike her mother, perhaps because she is of a younger more modern generation, Sheila doesn't seem as surprised by a man's bad behaviour; while Mrs Birling wants to stop the discussion, Sheila wants to hear more, partly to make Gerald suffer and partly to understand what he did and why.

Pages 10–11

Revise 1

1) Mrs Birling admits that Eva appealed to her charitable organisation for help.
2) The Inspector reveals that Eva was pregnant.
3) Mrs Birling states that the father of Eva's child is responsible for her death.
4) Mr and Mrs Birling begin to realise that Eric was the father of Eva's child.

Revise 2

Answers might include: a) dramatic irony as Mrs Birling doesn't realise she's criticising her own son; the way Sheila cuts her off and tries to stop her speaking as she's worked out that Eric is the father. b) Sheila using a rhetorical question to try to get her mother to realise that Eric is the father; Mrs Birling's slow realisation shown through the stage direction and the ellipses, and her words suggesting she doesn't want to believe the truth.

Revise 3

Answers might include: her prejudice based on class and status ('gross impertinence … prejudiced me'); her moral criticisms ('a girl in her position … a girl of that sort'); her arrogance ('I did nothing I'm ashamed of … I did my duty', 'I've done nothing wrong') and blaming of others ('Go and look for the father of the child. It's his responsibility.').

Comic Strip

I'm very sorry. But I think she had only herself to blame.

Extend

Answers might explore: both characters criticise Mrs Birling; Sheila is disgusted with her mother ('cruel and vile'); the Inspector is angry ('[very sternly] Her position now is that she lies with a burnt-out inside') and critical of her refusal to accept responsibility ('You're not even sorry now').

Pages 12–13

Revise 1

1) Eric reveals how he met Eva and got her pregnant.
2) Eric accuses Mrs Birling of killing Eva and her baby.
3) The Inspector reminds the Birling family that they are all responsible for Eva's death.
4) As he leaves, the Inspector states that all members of society need to look after each other.

Revise 2

Answers should include: a) Mrs Birling is shocked as she has always had a false impression of her son; she feels he has brought shame on the family; b) Mr Birling is disgusted by the story and wants to protect Sheila and his wife from hearing the details; c) the Inspector is critical of how Eric treated Eva, partly linked to her gender and her class.

Revise 3

Answers might focus on: the Inspector's use of an imperative ('Remember') shows the importance of the Birlings taking personal responsibility; the verb 'Remember' urges them to think about their actions and change; use of language to convey unity and social responsibility, emphasised by the short sentences and the rule of three; repetition of the plural pronoun 'we' suggests unity and mutual responsibility, relating to Priestley's socialist beliefs.

Comic Strip

'Because you're not the kind of father a chap could go to when he's in trouble.'

Extend

Answers might explore: his description of working-class lives, using a list for emphasis; the message that Eva's story is representing the story of 'millions of' other people; the prophetic image of the two world wars, emphasised by the tricolon, known to the audience but not the characters; possible image of a social revolution.

Pages 14–15

Revise 1

1) The Birlings start to suspect that the Inspector isn't a real policeman.
2) When Gerald returns, he reveals that the Inspector isn't a real policeman.
3) Mr and Mrs Birling and Gerald relax and want to forget about the evening's events.
4) The Birlings receive a phone call from the police.

Revise 2

Answers should include: **a)** Birling is more worried about his reputation than Eva's fate; **b)** Eric sees the irony of his father's behaviour at the start of the evening, realising how flawed his views are; Eric realises there is another way of viewing society, which challenges the views held by his father.

Revise 3

Answers might include: the stage directions show Birling joking about the events because he thinks they no longer personally affect him; he still thinks socialism is nonsense; his use of the verb 'kill' as part of his mockery emphasises his lack of a sense of responsibility; Sheila represents the new generation and her use of 'before' shows that the evening has changed her; the verb 'pretending' shows criticism of the way the others are ignoring the truth or their responsibilities.

Comic Strip

'Nonsense! You'll have a good laugh over it yet.'

Extend

Answers might explore: Eric's and Sheila's change of outlook and how disturbed they are by the others' behaviour; Mr and Mrs Birling and Gerald having a drink, as if continuing the evening from before the Inspector arrived; Birling's focus on his own status and the way he toasts the family; Mrs Birling viewing Sheila and Eric as childish; Birling and Gerald expecting Sheila to take back the engagement ring as if Gerald's affair never took place.

Pages 16–17

Revise 1

Mr Birling, Sheila, Gerald, Mrs Birling, Eric

Revise 2

Answers should include: **a)** at the end of Act 1, the audience has just found out that Gerald had an affair with Eva/Daisy; Sheila's repetition creates suspense by suggesting there's more scandal to come; the opening of her speech creates tension because she sounds scared; the Inspector's reappearance is drawn out to create suspense; his single-word question sounds dominant and threatening; **b)** at the end of Act 2, Mrs Birling's refusal to believe the truth contrasts with Sheila's understanding; the audience is also working out that Eric is the father; Eric's return to the stage is drawn out through sound and movement to create suspense.

Revise 3

Answers might include: Gerald's and Mr Birling's confidence and relaxed attitude, with references to engagements and jokes; the use of sound (the telephone ringing followed by a moment of silence) to create a shock; tension being built through Birling's changing facial expression and the pauses that break up his final speech; the final appearance of the characters on stage may lead the audience to consider their different levels of guilt; Priestley creates a memorable ending that encourages the audience to consider the questions raised about society and social responsibility.

Comic Strip

'My God! But – look here –'

Extend

Answers might explore: Gerald's sudden reaction when it is revealed that Eva changed her name to Daisy, the way he tries to cover up his reaction, and Sheila's response; Sheila's distress being heightened by the revelation that Eva was pregnant, and how this reflects on Mrs Birling; the dramatic irony of Mrs Birling condemning her own son, despite Sheila's protests, then the gradual realisation of Mr and Mrs Birling that Eric is the father.

Pages 18–19

Revise 1

Socialism	A belief in greater legal and financial equality and the importance of helping the poorest in society.
Capitalism	A belief in individual gain through hard work, the acceptance of inequality and the importance of profit.
Exploitation	Using someone unfairly for your (usually financial) benefit.

Revise 2

Suggested answers:
a) Upper class. The people in society with the most money and status; often established families with country homes, passing their money down through inheritance. The Crofts.
b) Middle class. People who have recently earned a lot of money, usually through a profession or setting up a successful business. The Birlings.
c) Working class. The people with least money and status; they are workers rather than employers; often linked to manual labour. Eva Smith.

Revise 3

Answers might explore: Birling's reference to 'we employers' shows he is middle class by the way he aligns himself with the employers, linking to him being a capitalist because he is setting himself apart from the workers; this is emphasised by the abstract noun 'prosperity' and the inference that he is only referring to the prosperity of the middle classes, not everyone in society, and he doesn't value the working class as people, just a resource; his reassurance, the noun phrase 'labour trouble' and the superlative adjective 'worst' suggest that he sees socialism and striking for better rights as a bad thing; the reference to 'Capital' shows he is a capitalist and his focus on individual gain can be seen in the phrase 'our interests'.

Extend

Answers might explore: he doesn't want to pay his workers more, even though he acknowledges they do a good job; his short sentence 'I refused, of course' suggests that he thinks it's a simple issue and that he can't be in the wrong; he refers to his 'duty' to keep costs down and profit up, showing his capitalist values; when he talks of the need to 'come down sharply' on workers, it shows he has the power and the right to punish them, as well as implying that he sees them as a resource to exploit.

Pages 20–21

Revise 1

a) True
b) False
c) False
d) True
e) True

Revise 2

Answers might include: All the quotations make use of dramatic irony; because the play is set in the past, the audience know things that Birling and the other characters do not. **a)** because the *Titanic* did sink (in 1912), the audience would realise that Birling isn't as wise as he thinks; the *Titanic* can also symbolise his family and reputation as it isn't as secure and stable as he believes; **b)** similarly, audience knowledge of two world wars and periods of economic depression undermine Birling's character; **c)** the Inspector's words link to the two world wars when men from different classes fought and died alongside each other; this was one of the reasons greater equality was achieved in the post-war years.

Revise 3

Answers might include: the use of verb phrases like 'turned her away ... refused her' criticise a lack of compassionate socialist values; the size of the requested wages increase suggests Eva wanted very little and that capitalist values are therefore selfish; the metaphor 'heavier price' links Eva's death to capitalism, repeating the language of economics to underline his moral point to Mr Birling and the audience; the contrast between the pronouns 'their' and 'we' accuses the Birlings of lacking social responsibility; his statements about 'We' use the rule of three to emphasise the importance of socialist values.

Extend

Answers might explore: the way in which Eric and Sheila question and criticise their parents while supporting each other; their empathy for Eva and guilt for their actions, compared to their parents' wish to cover up what has happened in order to save their own reputations; Sheila's and Eric's feelings that their lives have changed, compared to the other characters wanting to continue as before; the harsh and stubborn attitude of the parents, compared to their children's willingness to listen and change suggests to the audience that the younger generation are in the right.

Pages 22–23
Revise 1

Answers should include: 'counting their pennies' suggests they did not have much money so had to be very careful in order to survive financially; 'dingy little' suggests they could only afford small, dark, unattractive rooms to live in.

Revise 2

Answers should include: **a)** there are lots of working-class girls living in poor conditions; the lives of working-class girls weren't understood or empathised with by the middle classes (the Inspector's direct address, 'Miss Birling', indicates he is aware of Sheila's ignorance); the noun phrase 'cheap labour' suggests these girls are exploited because they're desperate for work; **b)** Gerald's description emphasises the poverty and poor living conditions of working-class girls; the verb phrase 'turned out' also relates to the lack of social welfare as Eva/Daisy is going to be made homeless.

Revise 3

Answers might explore: despite the Christian belief in caring for others, the adjectives 'deserving' and 'good' suggest Christian charities sat in judgement on the poor; it is implied that some charities only helped if the person in need seemed moral enough; the noun 'influence' emphasises Mrs Birling's abuse of the power she has over Eva, even though she claims to help people; the phrase 'great deal of useful work' shows she is proud of her charity work, implying she does it more for status than an actual desire to help other people.

Extend

Answers might explore: her disgust at Gerald's affair; her shock that Eric gets drunk; her shock that a respected local councillor (Alderman Meggarty) is a drunk and a womaniser; her disapproval of Eva being pregnant yet unmarried; her disapproval of the man who got Eva pregnant; her lack of human kindness for others ('INSPECTOR: She needed not only money but advice, sympathy, friendliness. You've had children. You must have known what she was feeling.'); Sheila's criticism of her 'cruel' behaviour; her refusal to accept any responsibility for her actions.

Pages 24–25
Revise 1

Answers might include: the doorbell interrupts Mr Birling just as the Inspector frequently interrupts him throughout the play; it interrupts him while he's being self-satisfied, which reflects how the Inspector's investigation challenges his selfish attitudes; the bell is sharp and shocking, in the same way that the Inspector is very precise and reveals shocking information.

Revise 2

Answers should include: **a)** the initial lighting suggests how the family are currently happy and seem to be closely united; this is supported by lines like 'BIRLING: It's one of the happiest nights of my life.' **b)** The 'brighter and harder' lighting links to how the Inspector exposes the different family secrets and forces the characters to see the consequences of their actions; this could be supported by phrases such as 'INSPECTOR: I'm not going until I know *all* that happened.'

Revise 3

Answers might focus on: the set as a whole reflects the Birlings' social status; the sturdy expensive furniture links to this as well as representing their confidence about their lives; the fact that the house is 'suburban' reminds us that the Birlings are middle class (rather than having a country mansion like the upper classes); the port, cigar box and champagne glasses reflect wealth, with the latter highlighting the difference between their life and Eva Smith's, who has drunk bleach.

Extend

Answers might include: 'GERALD: The governor prides himself on being a good judge of port' links to the port and champagne, suggesting they are drunk by wealthy people and reflects status; 'BIRLING: Tell cook from me' links to the dinner being cleared away, showing that the family are wealthy enough to have servants; 'MRS BIRLING: Arthur, what about this famous toast of yours?' links to the drinks glasses and how the Birlings are confident and satisfied with their lives; 'BIRLING: And we're in for a time of steadily increasing prosperity' relates to the general appearance of the set showing that he is confident about his life and future, and suggesting that his family are getting richer (at the expense of poor workers).

Pages 26–27
Revise 1

Answers should include five of the following:

INSPECTOR: She was <u>out of work</u> for the next two months. Both her <u>parents were dead</u> so that she'd <u>no home</u> to go back to. And she hadn't been able to save much out of what Birling and Company had paid her. So that after two months, with <u>no work</u>, <u>no money</u> coming in, and living in lodgings, with <u>no relatives to help</u> her, <u>few friends</u>, <u>lonely</u>, <u>half-starved</u>, she was feeling <u>desperate</u>.

Revise 2

Answers should include: **a)** the Inspector initially shows politeness and respect as would be expected; **b)** he begins to take charge of

the room and interrupts Birling – he's not intimidated by his social status; **c)** he begins to contradict the other characters' opinions, showing his more caring, socialist views.

Revise 3

Answers might explore: the Inspector continually asks questions; he cuts across Gerald's speech when it starts to move away from his interrogation of Sheila; he makes leading statements (such as 'you might be said to have been jealous of her') to expose Sheila's behaviour; he speaks '[harshly]' and '[sternly]'; his blunt descriptions of Eva's death.

Comic Strip

'Apologise for what – doing my duty?'

Extend

Answers might explore: the Inspector's lack of respect for the Birlings' social status, shown through dialogue and stage directions; his apportioning of blame; his open criticism of Mrs Birling; Priestley's message, delivered through the Inspector, that we must accept personal and social responsibility, and should care more about inequality.

Pages 28–29
Revise 1

Answers might include:

a) He is dominant: 'Are you listening, Sheila?'
b) He is self-important: 'And I'm talking as a hard-headed, practical man of business'
c) He is patronising: 'You've a lot to learn yet'
d) He has capitalist values: 'the interests of Capital – are properly protected'
e) He doesn't understand the world as well as he thinks he does: 'there isn't a chance of war'

Revise 2

Answers might include:

a) Mrs Birling: he loves his wife and doesn't mind being gently told off by her, 'Oh – come, come – I'm treating Gerald like one of the family'
b) Sheila: he likes her to be obedient, 'Are you listening, Sheila?'; he's patronising about women, 'clothes mean something quite different to a woman … token of their self-respect'
c) Eric: he patronises him and likes to lecture him, 'I wanted you to have the benefit of my experience'

Revise 3

Answers might focus on: the use of the title 'Lady Croft' shows his respect for people of a higher social status; the comparative adjective 'better' shows unwilling acceptance that he is below the Crofts in terms of status; he likes to boast of his social accomplishments, repeating the idea of being Lord Mayor (first to Gerald, then to the Inspector) and using a meeting with royalty to raise his sense of status; he is over-confident about his life ('[Laughs complacently]') and eager for greater status (the knighthood) as it will place him on a more equal standing with the Crofts.

Comic Strip

'working together – for lower costs and higher prices.'

Extend

Answers might explore: Birling cannot understand why his children have turned against him and aren't focused on avoiding scandal; he comes into particular conflict with Eric who goes against traditional family expectations and openly challenges his mother and father; he mocks their sense of guilt, seeing the younger generation's greater understanding of social responsibility as ridiculous.

Pages 30–31

Revise 1

Mrs Birling sees herself as **more important** than other people. She places herself above **young people** and the working class when speaking to Sheila: 'Please don't contradict me like that. And in any case, I don't suppose for a moment that we can understand why the girl committed suicide. Girls of that class –'. The **verb** 'contradict' shows she believes her views **have priority** while the phrase **'that class'** indicates disapproval of the poor. She is **dismissive** of Eva's suicide, convinced it has nothing to do with her family, and the phrase 'I don't suppose for a moment that we can understand' suggests her unwillingness to **empathise** with others.

Revise 2

Answers should include:

a) 'deserving' suggests that she is judgemental rather than compassionate and believes, because of her social status, that she has the right to judge others

b) 'prejudiced' shows she treated Eva unfairly but also that she feels this was justified

c) 'I'm very sorry' is shown to be insincere by the subsequent use of 'But' and placing any blame solely on Eva

d) she believes that working-class people and girls who are pregnant out of wedlock should behave in a humble and lowly way in order to receive help.

Revise 3

Answers might focus on: her disgust at Gerald's behaviour, showing her eagerness to judge him; her shock at hearing about Meggarty, revealing how she is unaware of what middle-class society is really like; her attempt to shield Sheila from the truth because of middle-class etiquette and her belief that Sheila is more innocent than she actually is; her words build up a picture of her morality, in order to show her hypocrisy once she is questioned herself.

Comic Strip

'Besides, you're not that type – you don't get drunk – '

Extend

Answers might explore: her apportioning of blame to the father, continuing her judgemental attitude and unwillingness to accept personal responsibility; her disbelief that her son could have got a girl pregnant because she sees the family as morally and socially superior; the distress shown in the stage directions as she realises what she has done; Priestley uses her to expose moral hypocrisy and a lack of compassion amongst the middle classes.

Pages 32–33

Revise 1

a) adverb – horribly

b) selfish – 'I wish you hadn't told me'

c) comparison – 'and I've been so happy'

d) curiosity – 'What was she like? Quite young?'

Revise 2

Answers should include: a) i) Gerald's affair; ii) her refusal to accept Gerald's behaviour and calling off the engagement; b) The Birlings' lifestyle isn't as secure and happy as they think it is.

Revise 3

Answers might explore: her criticism of her father's treatment of Eva, using the adjective 'mean'; initially following her father's advice that she did nothing wrong and instead focusing on how it's made her feel unhappy (the adjectives 'rotten' and 'worse'); her brief attempt to justify her behaviour ('it didn't seem to be anything very terrible at the time') followed by her repetition of 'never' to suggest she'll change her behaviour; her selfishness still appears through her comment that she can't go back to Milwards.

Comic Strip

'No, he's giving us rope – so that we'll hang ourselves.'

Extend

Answers might explore: at first, she focuses more on how bad she has been made to look, rather than Eva's death; she accepts blame and apologises but also refuses to accept sole responsibility; she summarises each character's culpability; she tries to make her mother more accepting of responsibility and criticises her treatment of Eva.

Pages 34–35

Revise 1

Answers might include:

a) 'If you think that's the best she can do –'

b) 'You're squiffy.'

c) 'Yes, I know – but still – '

d) '[She and Sheila and Eric go out]'

Revise 2

Answers should include: a) he admits to being drunk and aggressive, implying he forced himself on Eva; b) he found Eva attractive and enjoyed sex with her but didn't really care about her; c) he tried to do what was right but saw money as solving everything (reminding us that they were from different classes).

Revise 3

Answers might explore: he insults Sheila and this is highlighted by short sentences and spoken emphasis (through italics); Sheila stands up for herself and it is clear she has kept secrets for him; his repetition of the verb 'killed' is used to attack his mother and this is emphasised by the repetition of 'damn you' (perhaps having more impact in a religious family of the early 1900s); he uses contrasting verb phrases ('protect me'/'turned her away') to highlight how Eva was treated unfairly; the pauses in his speech show a mixture of distress and uncontrolled anger.

Comic Strip

'I hate these fat old tarts round the town – the ones I see some of your respectable friends with –'

Extend

Answers might explore: Eric openly challenges his father, contradicting expectations of family respect at the time; he increasingly gets his point of view across by shouting, leading Birling to do the same; it is clear that Birling blames Eric and is more worried about public scandal (and the loss of his potential knighthood) than the death of Eva and his son's feelings.

Pages 36–37

Revise 1

Answers should include: 'You couldn't have done anything else'; 'I should say so!'; 'Yes, I think you were. I know we'd have done the same thing.'

Revise 2

Answers should include: a) Gerald felt sorry for Eva; b) he was surprised by how poor/hungry she was and wanted to help; c) he found her somewhere to live out of compassion but this also made her reliant upon him and sex may have been all she could offer in return; d) although he made her happy, he also used her as a distraction (presumably having no intention of continuing the relationship because of her class).

Revise 3

Answers might include: Gerald cannot see the point of the Inspector's inquiries (for example, 'I don't really see that this inquiry gets you anywhere'); Gerald is offended by the Inspector's lack of politeness (given his social status); he is complacent about his life, believing he's never done anything wrong or that his secrets are safely hidden.

Comic Strip

'we're respectable citizens and not criminals.'

Extend

Answers might explore: Sheila is angry about the affair and enjoys Gerald being questioned; he thinks this is cruel of her; he doesn't fully apologise for the affair; there is the implication (partly through Birling's support) that it is acceptable for men to have sex out of wedlock but that it would be disgusting for Sheila to have done so; there is also the implication that working-class girls can be exploited for sex as well as labour; by the end of the questioning, the truth has been exposed about the affair and they have seen each other's true natures.

Pages 38–39

Revise 1

Answers should include: Mr Birling and Sheila both made her unemployed, financially desperate, and ultimately homeless; Gerald used her for sex then discarded her; Eric used her for sex, got her pregnant, and was too immature to support her; Mrs Birling refused her financial and emotional charity.

Revise 2

Answers should include: the Inspector sees the Birlings' actions as contributing to Eva's death but Mr Birling will not accept this viewpoint; Mrs Birling believes that working-class people, and girls pregnant out of wedlock, should behave in a humble way, and that Eva didn't deserve help; the Inspector believes people should be treated compassionately and Mrs Birling should feel guilty.

Revise 3

Answers might explore: both characters have economic power over Eva: Mr Birling sacks her, leaving her without pay and Mrs Birling refuses her application for charitable support; Mrs Birling also shows social power as she is head of the charity group and judges Eva morally.

Comic Strip

'Just used her … as if she was an animal, a thing, not a person.'

Extend

Answers might explore: the Inspector uses blunt and brutal descriptions of Eva's death to emphasise its horror; the characters are shown to have treated Eva unfairly, for example, Mr Birling's anger, Sheila's jealousy and Mrs Birling's moral hypocrisy; the Inspector's descriptions of her living conditions and lonely lifestyle contrast with that of the Birlings, showing the difference between the working and middle classes in the early 1900s; looking back at 1912, before a proper labour movement and the welfare state, it is clear that Eva is exploited and has no one to turn to.

Pages 40–41

Revise 1

Answers might include: the Inspector points out the need to show compassion for the working classes; he suggests the middle classes have the power to improve or destroy the lives of poorer people and that great social responsibility is needed; he highlights the need for socialist unity rather than selfishness.

Revise 2

Answers should include: **a)** Mrs Birling doesn't change her outlook, refusing to accept she's done anything wrong; **b)** Mr Birling also doesn't change his attitude, seeing socialism as ridiculous; **c)** Sheila changes her outlook, accepts guilt and tries to get others to do the same; **d)** Eric realises that his father's views are flawed and begins to challenge the ideas he's been brought up with.

Revise 3

Answers might include: Mr Birling is quick to blame Eric for the evening's events; he excuses his behaviour and that of his wife; he focuses on the possible effects of a public scandal and is more interested in losing out on a knighthood than Eva's death or Eric's feelings; towards the end of Act 3, he tries to avoid responsibility and pretend nothing has happened, contrasting with Eric's outlook.

Comic Strip

'You're beginning to pretend now that nothing's really happened at all.'

Extend

Answers should explore: Mr and Mrs Birling show they haven't changed by refusing to accept responsibility and then ridiculing what the Inspector has said to them; Gerald also hasn't changed, and is keen to prove the

Inspector was a hoax, suggesting that their actions may have affected different girls not just one so they shouldn't feel guilty, and expecting Sheila to resume their engagement; Eric and Sheila openly argue with their parents, showing that they have learnt from the Inspector; Priestley is criticising people who will not accept social responsibility while encouraging the audience to empathise with Sheila and Eric's views, representing the younger generation of 1912 that developed a more compassionate society.

Pages 42–43

Revise 1

GERALD: Old Joe Meggarty, <u>half-drunk</u> and <u>goggle-eyed</u> … He's a <u>notorious womaniser</u> as well as being one of the <u>worst sots</u> and <u>rogues</u> in Brumley.

Revise 2

Answers should include:

a) Envy: one of Sheila's reasons for having Eva sacked

b) Gluttony: the family's celebration; Eric's drinking

c) Greed: Birling's wish to keep costs down and profits high

d) Lust: Gerald's and Eric's affairs with Eva

e) Pride: Mrs Birling's charity work and refusal to admit she should have helped Eva

f) Sloth: Sheila's lazy way of life

g) Wrath: Birling's sacking of Eva and his conflict with the other characters; Sheila having Eva sacked

Revise 3

Answers might include: the middle-class complacency shown by Gerald in his contrasting nouns, showing he doesn't think the rich can be criminals (or, alternatively, that they are above the law); the way the Inspector contradicts Gerald through his phrase 'isn't as much difference', and his challenging of Gerald's outlook on society in 'you think'; challenging of class hierarchies increasing in the first decades of the 20th century.

Comic Strip

'I wasn't in love with her or anything.'

Extend

Answers might include: Mrs Birling looks down on Eva for having sinned by having sex out of wedlock; her dialogue also implies that she thinks all working-class people are in some way less moral than the middle and upper classes; the Inspector points out Mrs Birling's hypocritical lack of morality in not helping someone so clearly in need, and criticises the way in which she seems proud of her actions.

Pages 44–45

Revise 1

Answers should include: 'young' suggests the vulnerable aren't cared for enough; 'died' shows the fate of these people; 'agony' suggests how life is an unnecessary struggle, while 'couldn't go on' shows that people feel beaten by society rather than part of it.

Revise 2

Answers might include: **a)** Birling sees personal gain as the most important thing in society; the use of 'has to' suggests he cannot

see an alternative way of life; he doesn't see the need to care for others; **b)** his 'bees' simile suggests he sees ideas of unity and empathy as ridiculous and this is emphasised by the word 'nonsense'; his disparaging use of the phrase 'mixed up' implies that he sees himself as better than other people, believing in a social hierarchy rather than 'community'.

Revise 3

Answers might include: Priestley applies the popular socialist views of the 1940s to the Birlings in 1912; the Inspector's words emphasise the number of working-class people who are suffering due to exploitation; he repeats the plural pronoun 'We' to promote unity instead of competition, and this is highlighted in the images in his three short sentences; the reference to war – when different classes of Britain fought alongside each other – promotes the final reason why it is better to work together than against each other.

Comic Strip

'But she died in misery and agony – hating life –'

Extend

Answers might explore: the way the Inspector challenges Mr Birling's views; how the Inspector's arrival (the doorbell) symbolically interrupts Birling's celebration of the survival of the fittest; the use of references to Eva's death to regularly condemn selfish attitudes.

Pages 46–47

Revise 1

Answers should include: Social responsibility is the belief that we should help those people in society who are less fortunate than us and that individuals should be accountable for the impact of their actions on others.

Revise 2

Answers should include: **a)** Mr Birling's use of the insult 'cranks' shows he thinks social responsibility is ridiculous; he doesn't think you should 'look after' anyone but yourself; **b)** in contrast, the Inspector encourages empathy through the verb phrase 'put ourselves in the place'; he believes this makes you a better person ('do us all a bit of good').

Revise 3

Answers might explore: the use of the abstract noun 'guilt' to show responsibility; his use of the pronoun 'our' suggests that, as a member of society, the Inspector sees himself as partly to blame for Eva's death; the verb 'share', relating to socialist ideas of sharing and equality, shows the importance of joint responsibility; the use of a list emphasises all the different ways in which social responsibility can be shown, perhaps linking to the establishment of the welfare state in the 1940s.

Comic Strip

'You must have known what she was feeling. And you slammed the door in her face.'

Extend

Answers might explore: Gerald accepts the things they have all done but doesn't think it matters because there isn't a suicide to be blamed for; he believes they've affected the lives of several different women not one, suggesting that makes things better rather than worse; he feels confident that their reputations are safe and this is more important to him than the effects of their actions on individuals.

Pages 48–49
Revise 1
Answers should include: Personal responsibility means accepting the consequences of your actions.

Revise 2
Answers should include: a) the verb 'blame' shows Birling is unwilling to accept responsibility and wants to accuse others; b) 'fact' shows that Eric isn't hiding from his personal responsibility and this is emphasised by the parallelism of 'I did what I did' to show that it can't be ignored or forgotten; c) Sheila's use of the verbs 'dodging and pretending' show her criticism of her parents for trying to avoid their responsibility, while the phrase 'Between us we …' uses a plural pronoun to admit her responsibility and make others accept theirs.

Revise 3
Answers might explore: her use of the verb 'confess' to show acceptance of guilt; the italics in 'was true' to suggest spoken emphasis that they can't ignore what they did; the use of the rhetorical question encourages others to agree; a list of verb phrases is used to summarise the actions they should feel responsible for; the phrase 'finished her' shows Sheila refusing to ignore the ultimate consequences of her own actions.

Comic Strip
'He certainly didn't make me confess – as you call it.'

Extend
Answers might explore: Mr Birling's focus on his reputation, blaming the others for admitting what they'd done, and his attitude after they contact the hospital; Mrs Birling's stubborn refusal to accept that she did anything wrong; Gerald's belief that the Inspector was actually talking about several girls and how that somehow means they're less responsible.

Pages 50–51
Revise 1
Answers might include: '[champagne glasses]'; 'BIRLING: I'm still on the Bench'; 'MRS BIRLING: All right, Edna. I'll ring from the drawing room when we want coffee'; 'BIRLING: … this public-school-and-Varsity life you've had …'; 'SHEILA: … I'd persuade mother to close our account with them.'

Revise 2
Answers should include: Birling places profit above the welfare of his workers; the phrase 'come down' shows he believes the workers are below him; the adverb 'sharply' suggests Birling sees harsh treatment and inequality as necessary for a good business; the phrase 'asking the earth' shows Birling thinks that if he gives in to workers, there will be no end to their demands in future, and also implies

a fear that moves to solve inequality would adversely affect the quality of his own life.

Revise 3
Answers might include: the reference to 'women of the town' suggests prostitutes, relating to Gerald's male economic power and Eva's economic vulnerability; she has no parents, whereas Gerald's are wealthy people of status; she's unemployed while it is implied that Gerald has been at work; the adverbs 'desperately' and 'actually' suggest his surprise at her lack of money while he is able to buy the drinks and has enough status to have 'made' the people at the hotel 'find some food for her'; Eva is about to be evicted from her 'miserable' single room whereas Gerald has a friend who has left his well-located apartment empty while he goes away for six months.

Comic Strip
'But these girls aren't cheap labour – they're people.'

Extend
Answers might explore: what the Inspector says to Sheila to get her to understand Eva's life and death in Act 1; his criticism in Act 2 of how Mrs Birling treated Eva; his final speeches in Act 3.

Pages 52–53
Revise 1
Answers should include: the mother tries to control her two children; Sheila and Eric are bickering childishly, each one trying to make the other look bad in front of their mother; Mrs Birling criticises Sheila's youthful way of talking then tells them to stop arguing.

Revise 2
Answers might include: Mr Birling doesn't value Eric's opinions and interrupts him to stop him getting in the way of his speech, 'Just let me finish, Eric. You've a lot to learn yet.'; he tells Sheila off for not paying enough attention to his speech, 'Are you listening, Sheila?', and she obediently apologises, 'I'm sorry, Daddy.'

Revise 3
Answers might include: traditional expectations of parent–child relationships and levels of respect being overturned; Eric and Mr Birling conflicting over Eric having a drink; Eric telling his father that he's not approachable and Mr Birling reacting angrily; Eric accusing his mother of killing Eva; Mr and Mrs Birling accusing Sheila of not loyal enough to the family; Mr Birling angrily sending Sheila out of the room.

Comic Strip
'And I say the girl's dead and we all helped to kill her – and that's what matters –'

Extend
Answers might explore: Priestley suggests there is hope for the future as the young can change; looking back to 1912 from 1945, he is praising a generation that broke away from their parents' attitudes and developed a more caring outlook on society; Sheila and Eric agree with each other as they accuse Mr Birling of not learning anything; Sheila and Eric stand up to their father when he threatens to send

Sheila to her room; Sheila and Eric disagree with their parents over whether it matters if the Inspector wasn't a real policeman; Eric supports Sheila when she criticises her father and Gerald for acting as if nothing has happened; Sheila and Eric think about the Inspector's final words and are disturbed by their parents' attitude.

Pages 54–55
Revise 1
Answers should include: the short time-frame intensifies the action, keeping the focus on the consequences of the characters' actions.

Revise 2
Answers might include: a) 'SHEILA: [She almost breaks down, but just controls herself] How could I know what would happen afterwards?'; b) 'GERALD: So – for God's sake – don't say anything to the Inspector.'; c) 'MRS BIRLING: [with a cry] Oh – Eric – how could you?'; d) 'MR BIRLING: There'll be a pubic scandal.'

Revise 3
Answers might include: 'MRS BIRLING: he certainly didn't make me confess – as you call it.'; her use of the adverb 'certainly' emphasises her refusal to see that she's done anything wrong; this is added to by the additional phrase 'as you call it' to describe the verb 'confess', showing she doesn't believe she has said anything for which she should feel guilty; 'SHEILA: Everything we said had happened really had happened.'; repetition shows her acceptance of the past and this is emphasised by the adverb 'really'.

Comic Strip
'and that you're going to spend the rest of your life regretting it.'

Extend
Answers might explore: the Inspector's repetition of the imperative 'remember' in his final speeches; his short but vivid descriptions of Eva's death; his different tones of voice when speaking to characters about the past, such as '[savagely]' to Mr Birling or '[very deliberately]' to Mrs Birling.

Pages 56–57
Revise 1
Answers should include: Gerald has had an affair; Gerald and Sheila's relationship seems to be partly based around money and social standing (the ring, her lifestyle, reasons for father's approval); the engagement is called off; Gerald and Eric didn't love Eva/Daisy; in addition to a lack of romantic love, there is some lack of parental love and a lack of love for other people in society.

Revise 2
Answers should include: a) Sheila's dialogue jokes that Gerald is lying to her, foreshadowing the truth being revealed about his affair and how he has abused Sheila's trust; b) Gerald's toast sounds uncertain ('hope') and this links to the fact that he won't make her happy; the verb 'deserve' also implies that Sheila not getting her happy ending is partly a punishment for how she treated Eva; c) Sheila's exaggerated

comment about the ring foreshadows the moment when she returns it to Gerald.

Revise 3

Answers might include: Gerald makes it clear that Eva/Daisy felt more for him than he did for her; the phrase 'intensely grateful' adds an imbalance to the relationship, as Gerald has economic power so she needs him more than he needs her; while she was a brief distraction from work ('for a time'), he offered her a better, almost fantasy, life (Sheila's 'Fairy Prince' metaphor); both knew that the affair wouldn't last but she wanted it to (the adjective 'gallant' shows she accepted the break-up but wasn't happy about it).

Comic Strip

'Everything's alright now, Sheila. What about this ring?'

Extend

Answers might include: Gerald doesn't fully apologise to Sheila in Act 2; in Act 3, once they believe Eva isn't dead, Gerald expects Sheila to resume their engagement, even though he still had an affair; Mr Birling tries to stop Sheila breaking off the engagement in Act 2 and encourages her to resume the engagement in Act 3; he supports Gerald because he is the right class to marry Sheila and will add to Mr Birling's own social status as well as possibly being good for business, through links to Sir George Croft's factory; it might also be implied that Mr Birling sympathises with Gerald because he has done the same (Mrs Birling refers to her husband being similarly busy to Gerald, and many of Mr Birling's respectable friends appear to be having affairs).

Pages 58–73

Exam Practice

Use the mark scheme below to self-assess your strengths and weaknesses. Work up from the bottom, putting a tick by things you have fully accomplished, a ½ by skills that are in place but need securing, and underlining areas that need particular development. The estimated grade boundaries are included so you can assess your progress towards your target grade.

Pages 58–59

Answers might explore: the Inspector's dominant and rude attitude towards

Mr Birling, contrasting with expected behaviour in the early 1900s due to differing social status; the Inspector's lack of objectivity, especially when speaking to Mrs Birling in Act 2; his secrecy with the photograph, for example with Gerald in Act 1; the way the characters question who he was after he leaves in Act 3; the symbolic use of lighting and the surname Goole ('Ghoul') to suggest the character is more than just an Inspector, possibly a representation of social conscience.

Pages 60–61

Answers might explore: Birling being presented as a traditional middle-class patriarch of the early 1900s; his dominant behaviour in the first half of Act 1, relating also to the different roles of power he has undertaken in the community; his conflict with the Inspector throughout the play; how he responds when his children start to stand up to him, especially in Act 3; alternatively, the interactions between Mr and Mrs Birling in the first half of Act 1 suggest he is used to her challenging his lack of etiquette (linking to her being of a higher social status).

Pages 62–63

Answers might explore: the apparent easy and 'playful' nature of their relationship gradually revealing secrets, such as Gerald's mysterious behaviour during the previous summer; their relationship being partly based on class and economy – she clearly appreciates his wealth and Mr Birling approves of how it could benefit his business and social status (due to Gerald's higher class); Gerald's affair and how he and Birling try to forget about it, showing the imbalance of expectations in a relationship in the early 1900s; Sheila increasingly realising that she and Gerald are different from the people they thought they were.

Pages 64–65

Answers might explore: examples of what Mrs Birling believes to be Christian morality, such as how she judges Gerald's behaviour and her pride in her charity work; the Inspector showing that instead of being moral she is judgemental and cruel, through her treatment of Eva (linking to attitudes to the working classes and ideas of sin in the early 1900s); her sense of morality being undermined by the truth about Eric.

Pages 66–67

Answers might explore: social and personal responsibility; the refusal of Mr and Mrs Birling to accept responsibility (linked to his capitalist values and her twisted sense of morality); Gerald's avoidance of responsibility, especially in Act 3; Sheila's and Eric's attitudes to responsibility changing from Act 1 to Act 3 as they begin to adopt the Inspector's views rather than those of their parents (relating to the younger generation that pushed for a more caring society, paving the way for the socialism of the 1940s).

Pages 68–69

Answers might explore: inequality is one of the main themes of the play, especially in terms of attitudes towards inequality and also its consequences; contrast between the Birlings' life and Eva's (linking to class structures of the early 1900s); the contrast between Gerald's life and Eva's; the different degrees of power that the characters have over Eva (relating to the lack of welfare state and exploitation of the working class); the Inspector's message about inequality in Act 3, linking to popular socialist beliefs of the 1940s.

Pages 70–71

Answers might explore: the idea that respectability is a sham; Gerald complacently suggesting he's not a criminal because he's a 'respectable citizen' and the Inspector's response in Act 1; Gerald's and Eric's stories revealing the truth about Mr Birling's apparently respectable friends in Acts 2 and 3; Mr Birling's desperation to avoid any public scandal in Act 3.

Pages 72–73

Answers might explore: the play is about the revealing of secrets and lies, and the need to accept the truth of one's actions; Priestley exposes the truth about middle-class behaviour; Gerald's lies to Sheila and his desperation to keep the truth from the Inspector at the end of Act 1; Eric's secrets and lies, getting a girl pregnant and stealing from the family business; the idea that the older characters lie to themselves about their responsibility for Eva's death; Sheila and Eric trying to get the others to face the truth at the end, rather than pretend nothing has happened; the role of the Inspector in exposing the truth.

Grade	AO1 (12 marks)	AO2 (12 marks)	AO3 (6 marks)	AO4 (4 marks)
6–7+ (19–34 marks)	A convincing, well-structured essay that answers the question fully. Quotations and references are well chosen and integrated into sentences. The response covers the whole play.	Analysis of the full range of Priestley's methods. Thorough exploration of the effects of these methods. Accurate range of subject terminology.	Exploration is linked to specific aspects of the play's contexts to show a detailed understanding.	Consistently high level of accuracy. Vocabulary and sentences are used to make ideas clear and precise.
4–5 (13–18 marks)	A clear essay that always focuses on the exam question. Quotations and references support ideas effectively. The response refers to different points in the play.	Explanation of Priestley's different methods. Clear understanding of the effects of these methods. Accurate use of subject terminology.	References to relevant aspects of context show a clear understanding.	Good level of accuracy. Vocabulary and sentences help to keep ideas clear.
2–3 (6–12 marks)	The essay has some good ideas that are mostly relevant. Some quotations and references are used to support the ideas.	Identification of some different methods used by Priestley to convey meaning. Some subject terminology.	Some awareness of how ideas in the play link to its context.	Reasonable level of accuracy. Errors do not get in the way of the essay making sense.